THE TIGER

Look for these and other books in the
Lucent Endangered Animals and Habitats series:

The Amazon Rain Forest
The Bald Eagle
The Elephant
The Giant Panda
The Oceans
The Rhinoceros
Seals and Sea Lions
The Shark
The Tiger
The Whale
The Wolf

Other related titles in the Lucent Overview series:

Acid Rain
Endangered Species
Energy Alternatives
Garbage
The Greenhouse Effect
Hazardous Waste
Ocean Pollution
Oil Spills
Ozone
Pesticides
Population
Rainforests
Recycling
Vanishing Wetlands
Zoos

THE TIGER

BY STUART P. LEVINE

Endangered
Animals &
Habitats

LUCENT BOOKS, INC.
SAN DIEGO, CALIFORNIA

Library of Congress Cataloging-in-Publication Data

Levine, Stuart P., 1968–
    The tiger / Stuart P. Levine.
        p.   cm. — (Endangered animals & habitats)
    Includes bibliographical references (p.   ) and index.
    Summary: Discusses the various species of tigers and their
behavior and examines how they have become endangered through
habitat loss, hunting, research, and captivity.
    ISBN 1-56006-465-X (lib. : alk. paper)
    1. Tigers—Juvenile literature.   2. Endangered species—Juvenile
literature. [1. Tigers. 2. Endangered species.] I. Title. II. Series.
QL737.C23L474   1999
599.756—dc21   98-27237
                                                CIP
                                                AC

Copyright © 1999 by Lucent Books, Inc.
P.O. Box 289011, San Diego, CA 92198-9011
Printed in the U.S.A.

Contents

Introduction

THE TIGER OCCUPIES a special place in the minds and memories of most people in the world. Whether it was a favorite stuffed animal, a cartoon character, or an exciting live encounter at the local zoo, everyone has some connection to the world's largest feline. Powerful, mysterious, and beautiful, the tiger evokes both an overwhelming admiration for nature and primal fear.

Tigers used to range from the Russian far east through China, southeast Asia, India, and into Pakistan, as well as in the Caspian Sea region and a large chain of islands down through Indonesia. Today, however, they are found only in scattered isolated patches of forest throughout a small fraction of these areas. One hundred years ago there were over one hundred thousand tigers. Today, estimates range from five to seven thousand. The world has lost 95 percent of its tiger population during this century.

There is little mystery about how this happened. The human race has increased by leaps and bounds. In the last twenty years more people have lived on earth than in the planet's entire history. All these people have an enormous impact on the world's biological resources. And the population explosion has been most severe in the tiger's particular part of the world: Asia. For generations, local forest-dwelling people have lived off the land and only took what they needed to survive. Today, with more mouths to feed and cattle to graze, the average Asian farmer is forced to usurp more and more pristine land. Consequently, the tiger is pushed farther back into shrinking pockets, or islands, of forest. Without the ability to roam and interbreed with other local populations, the tiger has become a genetically poor species.

Habitat loss is not the only factor leading to the decline of the tiger. Poaching, or illegal hunting, has become a larger problem than ever before. In the days of old, the tiger hunt was conducted by powerful and glamorous kings and maharajas. Today, the average tiger hunter is a poverty-stricken native villager struggling with homelessness and the starvation of his family. While kings were few and far between, there is no shortage of poor local villagers in Asia today. With the prospect of earning a month's or even a year's wages by shooting one tiger, many of these people simply cannot resist. According to Valmik Thapar, a well-known journalist and conservationist, "A tiger a day" is shot and killed somewhere in Asia.

An increase in human population has led to a dramatic decrease in the world's tiger populations.

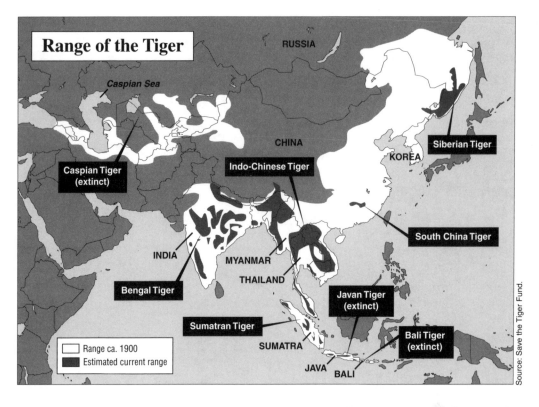

Range of the Tiger

RUSSIA

Caspian Sea

CHINA

Siberian Tiger

KOREA

Caspian Tiger
(extinct)

Indo-Chinese Tiger

South China Tiger

INDIA

MYANMAR

THAILAND

Bengal Tiger

Javan Tiger
(extinct)

Sumatran Tiger

Bali Tiger
(extinct)

SUMATRA

JAVA

BALI

☐ Range ca. 1900
■ Estimated current range

Source: Save the Tiger Fund.

In recent years, an unprecedented amount of research and conservation planning has been focused on the tiger. Scientists from all corners of the globe have come together to try to "stop the hemorrhaging," and prevent the rapidly approaching extinction of the tiger. Public awareness has helped to finance these projects and spur the governments of the world into action. But will it be enough? According to the Chinese calendar, 1998 is the Year of the Tiger. This calendar goes in cycles, repeating itself every twelve years. It is uncertain at this point whether the animal name given to the year 2010 will represent a creature lost to the wild forever.

1

What Is a Tiger?

THE TIGER IS perhaps one of the world's most admired and feared animals. It is a creature of great beauty, but capable of terrifying destruction. While most of the world today has been fortunate enough to see live tigers at a local zoo or a passing circus, most people have little understanding of a tiger's life in the wild. For many years, even centuries, the tiger was thought of as a murderous beast, devoid of compassion, existing only for the pure pleasure of the kill. In recent years, researchers have revealed a more complex picture of tigers. It is only during this last century that humans have become more familiar with the physiology, behavior, and environmental importance of the tiger. Coincidentally, it is also during this last century that the wild tiger's population has suffered a staggering drop, and now faces the very real threat of extinction.

Evolution of the tiger

Sixty-five million years ago the dinosaur ruled supreme on the earth. Of course, many other types of animals existed in its shadow, struggling to survive and waiting for the opportunity to climb the evolutionary ladder. One such group was the Miacids, small civetlike mammals, which, because of competition from the dinosaurs, were forced to survive on insects and very small prey. When the dinosaurs died out, the Miacids were left with an abundance of prey and little competition. They flourished and evolved into hundreds of species over the millennia. While most of these species have come and gone, today approximately two hundred remain. Collectively, the Miacids' descendants are known as carnivores. Animals that fall into the scientific classification of Carnivora are characterized by the possession of carnassial teeth: rear teeth that come together in a scissorlike motion in order to shear meat. Carnivora is a very diverse order, having members ranging from polar bears to weasels. Within this order exist several distinct families. All cats belong to the Felidae family. The first member of this particular family, which arrived about 36 million years ago, is known as the Dinictis. From Dinictis arose two separate lines of cat: the stabbing cats and the biting cats. The stabbers had weaker jaws and relied on long teeth to inflict fatal wounds, while the biters had very powerful jaws that they used to strangle or snap the neck of their prey. Perhaps the most famous of the stabbing cats was the saber-toothed. Often referred to as the saber-toothed tiger, it is in fact not very closely related to the tiger. The entire line of stabbing cats died out just under a

The tiger has an ancient heritage. The earliest-known fossil records indicate that the species dates back at least one million years.

million years ago. Today all felines are of the biting cat branch. The Felidae family is currently made up of thirty-seven distinct species, including the tiger.

The earliest fossils of tigers date back nearly a million years and were found near the Lena River in southeast Siberia. Most people think tigers need the comforts of a steamy tropical jungle to survive. It turns out, however, that the tiger originated in the snow-covered forests of northern Asia. Today a small population of tigers still exists in Siberia, but over a period of thousands of years, the tiger has migrated south and west to inhabit territories stretching from Turkey to the Javan Islands. As the tiger population spread, it differentiated into a number of distinct subspecies, or races. Today scientists recognize eight separate subspecies.

What's in a name?

Perhaps the most well known of the tiger subspecies is the Bengal tiger (*Panthera tigris tigris*). Sometimes referred to as the Indian tiger, its range extends from the southern tip of India up through most of the remaining forested regions of Pakistan and Myanmar. It is, by comparison, a midsize tiger, measuring an average length of ten feet. The Bengal possesses short fur and a deep, richly colored coat. It is the most plentiful of all the remaining races. It is estimated that about four thousand wild Bengals are left in the world. While this is considerably more than all the other races combined, the Bengal tiger is still in great danger: At the turn of the century, much of the Indian subcontinent was covered in dense jungle and an estimated forty thousand tigers existed in residence. It is not surprising that the vast majority of all tiger behavior and conservation research has been conducted on this subspecies. In addition to there being many more of them to study, the Bengal tiger, unlike some of its relatives, lives predominantly in a country that has been open to Western researchers for many years.

The Siberian tiger (*Panthera tigris altaica*) is another well-known subspecies. This cat, while numbering fewer than four hundred in the wild, is represented quite well in American and European zoos. The Siberian is the largest of all the subspecies, measuring up to thirteen feet long and weighing as much as 750 pounds. In fact, it is the largest type of cat on earth. It is easily distinguished from all other tigers by its stocky frame, huge head, and long, thick fur. The thick coat and large body mass provide Siberians with better heat retention than other tiger races, which is most likely an adaptation to the extremely cold climate they live in. They typically have a lighter colored coat, with more white present. Once found all throughout southeast Russia and northeast China, today this tiger exists only in one small province near Siberia.

The South China tiger (*Panthera tigris amoyensis*) has existed in both forests and rocky mountain habitats of southern China. Slightly smaller than the Bengal, it has fewer stripes, which are short and broad. The traditional Chinese practice of using tiger parts in religious ceremonies and medicine has led to a serious decline in this tiger population. Today, it is known to exist primarily in one small mountainous region bordering the Hunan province. Researchers estimate that as few as twenty to thirty South China tigers remain in the wild.

The fourth subspecies is the Malayan, or Indo-Chinese, tiger (*Panthera tigris corbetti*). It ranges through the dense jungles of Malaya, Thailand, Myanmar, and parts of Indochina. *P. t. corbetti* was only recognized as a separate subspecies from the Bengal in 1968. It is noticeably smaller and darker, and has short, narrow stripes. A lack of much formal research on this race has led to an unclear population count. However, according to Peter Jackson, a well-known tiger researcher, there may be about seventeen hundred of them in the wild today. Some scientists theorize that, many years ago, the Malayan tiger made the swim across the ocean straits to reach Indonesia, where three other distinct island subspecies developed.

The Sumatran (*Panthera tigris sumatrae*), found only on the island of Sumatra, is the smallest of the world's remaining tigers. It averages only eight feet in length. Its smaller stature is probably due to being isolated on an island. Typically, smaller, less numerous prey are available on an island. Consequently, smaller animals with smaller appetites are better adapted for survival. Sumatrans are also much darker than their northern counterparts, with more red in their coat, and have broad, black stripes, which are

The Indo-Chinese tiger is smaller than other tiger subspecies. It is recognizable by its darker color and short, narrow stripes.

often doubled. Poaching on the island is still widespread, and estimates for *P. t. sumatrae*'s population come in at less than one thousand. The three remaining subspecies of tiger—Caspian (*Panthera tigris virgata*), Javan (*Panthera tigris sondaica*), and Bali (*Panthera tigris balica*)—have been classified as extinct. They now exist only in fossils and photographs. The Caspian tiger was found throughout eastern Turkey, Iran, northern Iraq, parts of Russia, and Afghanistan. It was approximately the same size as the Bengal, though it had more stripes and very long fur on the underside of its body. The Javan tiger still existed in fair numbers after World War II, but by the 1970s, it remained in only one preserve on the southeast corner of the island. In 1980, tracks of at least three cats were found, but today researchers can find no signs of live tigers anywhere on the island.

The origin of the Bali tiger has long been a subject for debate among scientists. Some believe the tiger never occurred naturally on that particular island, and was instead brought in by human settlers. Others disagree, saying that the Javan tiger most likely swam the 1.5-mile channel to Bali many centuries ago, creating a new race. It did, however, gain recognition as a separate subspecies in 1912. The Bali tiger is thought to have lived as recently as the 1930s or 1940s. Since then, there have been reports of tigers seen on Bali, but none of these claims has ever been substantiated.

Mating and breeding

No matter the subspecies, some aspects of a tiger's life seem to remain constant. Tigers are solitary creatures. They typically live by themselves and only form pairs to mate. A male tiger's territory will overlap the territories of one or more females (depending on his size and strength). When a female comes into her breeding cycle, or estrus, all nearby males are immediately alerted by a number of signals.

During the estrous cycle the female becomes extremely agitated. She will appear restless, vocalize almost continu-

Although tigers are generally solitary creatures, male and females form temporary pairs when it is time to mate.

ously, and move around in determined pursuit of a mate. The vocalizations are typically enough to alert the male, but the female has other methods as well. All tigers will leave a scent mark on trees and plants to let other tigers know they have been there. The mark consists of a combination of urine and secretions from an anal gland. During estrus, the female's hormone levels cause the scent mark to smell very distinct. Male tigers coming across such a mark will actively try to locate its creator. If the female is not successful in attracting a mate, she will go out of estrus, and begin cycling again in a few weeks.

If the female tiger is successful in her mission, one or more males will begin to follow her. If there is more than one male involved, they will typically fight for breeding rights. Rarely is a tiger killed in such an encounter, but the larger and stronger male will usually win the battle, while the loser retreats. The winner will mate with the female. On one occasion, Valmik Thapar reported witnessing a third male hiding in the shadows. This hidden competitor waited for the loser to retreat and then attacked the winner, easily defeating the winded champion. The third male then enjoyed the spoils of his well-planned victory.

Once the pair are alone, they go through a very ritualistic courtship display. The tigers circle each other, growling

Facts About Tigers

Subspecies	Average Length	Average Weight
Bengal	8.8–10.2 ft.	419–569 lbs.
Indo-Chinese	8.4–9.3 ft.	330–430 lbs.
Siberian	8.8–10.8 ft.	419–675 lbs.
South China	7.6–8.7 ft.	287–386 lbs.
Sumatran	7.3–8.3 ft.	221–309 lbs.

*All statistics are for male tigers

Source: Save the Tiger Fund.

and vocalizing. As they get closer, they start nudging each other, rubbing bodies, and nuzzling faces. Eventually, the female will lay down to be mounted. When copulation is complete, the tigress will immediately roar and spin around to swipe at her mate. The male must move quickly to avoid getting hurt. Copulation will then be repeated. It will occur frequently, as often as every fifteen to twenty minutes, for three to six days. During this time neither tiger will go out to hunt. This frequent copulation significantly increases the chances of the female becoming pregnant. Once this process is complete, the male wanders off, leaving the female to care for the young.

Raising the young

After a pregnancy, or gestation period, of just over three months, the tigress will give birth. She will continue to hunt and remain active until just a few hours before she goes into labor. However, during the last few days of her pregnancy, she will spend a large amount of time scouring her territory for a suitable place to give birth. As a solitary animal, the tigress has no protection during this extremely vulnerable period. She must, therefore, find a well-hidden cave, outcropping of rock, or thick bush in which to seclude herself. Once she has chosen a spot, she spends several days familiarizing herself with every inch of the terrain. The tigress is very good at finding a hiding spot. No wild tiger has ever been observed giving birth. In fact, there have only been a handful of occasions where researchers have witnessed wild cubs younger than four to five months.

Delivery of the young can take as long as twenty-four hours, and typically results in a litter of two to five cubs. Each cub will weigh about three pounds. After delivery, the mother is completely exhausted and will not move for hours. The last thing she does before resting is eat the placenta and amniotic sacs. By doing this, she hides the smell of the birth from hungry predators, and provides herself with much-needed nourishment. The first few days of the cubs' lives are an extremely vulnerable time for them. They are blind for up to two weeks and completely helpless. The tigress will not leave her den for several days. She remains constantly vigilant, ignoring even her own need for food. She spends all of her time suckling her young and licking them to promote proper circulation and

A pair of captive-bred cubs nurse from their mother. After a female tiger gives birth, she will spend several days tending to her young, even at the expense of feeding herself.

bowel movements. After a time, the tigress will need to go out and hunt, as she must nourish herself to continue providing milk for her cubs.

At the beginning she will always hunt in the near vicinity of her den. The cubs' mortality rate is very high during this period, and the mother is very cautious and protective. She will be exceptionally aggressive toward any animal that comes near her while she is out hunting and will attempt to drive any predator (or human) away from the area at any cost. Despite all the mother's efforts, only one out of every two cubs typically reaches maturity.

As the weeks pass, the cubs continue to grow. They become more active with each other and their mother. At this point the tigress will begin bringing back chunks of meat to the den. As the cubs get better at eating solid foods, she will drag entire carcasses back with her, tearing open the kill and letting the cubs feed themselves. At about two to three months, the cubs will begin exploring their immediate surroundings. They will always be accompanied by their mother during these excursions, and any overzealous wandering will be met with a quick rebuke. As the cubs grow larger, the tigress will allow them to explore further to familiarize themselves with the forest in which they are going to live. By six months, the tigers are very rambunctious and spend a lot of time playing and wrestling with each other. This play behavior is a crucial part of developing their coordination and the skills they will need to hunt and survive on their own. Under the cover of night, the growing cubs will spend more time exploring. At this point the tigress hunts almost continuously, as her young are growing quickly (about half a pound a day) and need a constant supply of meat to eat. She never wanders far, but she must leave the cubs behind when she hunts because they are too wild and get in the way of her hunting. Eventually, she will take the young out with her to begin learning the mechanics of the hunt. They

A Siberian tiger cub. Young tigers are extremely weak and vulnerable to predators. Typically, only half a litter will survive to maturity.

must learn to remain silent and still. It is at this point that the tigress begins to deliver some stiff discipline. If the cubs make noise while observing the tigress's hunt, she will offer up a growl or a solid swipe at a tender nose.

Hunting is not easy, as the prey are very well adapted for survival. The teaching process lasts well over a year. When the cubs are ready to begin hunting, the tigress will start by injuring some prey and letting the cubs finish it off. Eventually, she will allow the cubs to begin and end the job themselves, lending a hand only when necessary. At about eighteen months, the tigress will begin to disappear for a few days at a time. She will return periodically to make sure her young are getting enough to eat. As the months pass, however, she will stay away for longer periods, until eventually she does not return at all. At this point the litter mates will remain together, hunting and playing, for anywhere from a few weeks to several months. Eventually, each cub will go off on its own to establish a territory and live the life of an adult tiger.

Tiger cubs play and wrestle to gain strength and agility. When the cubs are old enough, they will venture out to explore their environment and to join their mother on hunts.

Territories

Establishing a territory is one of the most important things an adult tiger must do in its life. This territory is the only place it will be allowed to hunt and breed without competition from other tigers. Territories range in size depending on several factors, including habitat, prey density, gender, and prowess. In an area such as India or Nepal, where there is a high concentration of prey, a male's range might be anywhere from 20 to 386 square miles. In Siberia, however, the climate is harsher and prey is less abundant. In these areas, a male's range may be from 200 to 1,500 square miles. The size of an individual's territory, within these ranges, will usually depend on the tiger's size, strength, and ability to defend its hunting grounds against neighboring tigers. A hungry tiger will seek to challenge others in order to gain better territory. The more common threat, however, comes from young tigers.

A Sumatran tiger prowls through the tall grass of its territory. Tigers have to be strong enough to wrest territory from other tigers and then defend it.

As a young male enters maturity and goes off on his own, he must seek out and establish his own territory. He will usually do this by choosing a suitable area and stalking the fringes of an established male's territory. The young tiger will hunt on the outskirts for quite some time, watching and assessing the area's primary occupant. Eventually, he will move in and attempt to wrest control of the area from the resident tiger. This usually involves a display of physical strength. Loud roaring and a heated battle are typically observed. If defeated, the youngster will move on to a new area, and try again. If successful, the older tiger will have to leave and attempt to displace someone else. Young tigers often roam as nomads for several years before they are strong enough and skilled enough to take control of their own territory. During these years, they are tolerated on the fringes of other cats' territories, as long as they keep their distance and do not attempt to mate with any of the local females.

Tigresses also establish a territory for themselves, but it is typically very different from a male's. A tigress will establish herself in a subsection of a male's larger territory. She is tolerated within his area because the male tiger knows that she will eventually provide him with the opportunity to mate. A male may have anywhere from one to seven females within his territory, again depending on his size and strength.

Though tigers are typically solitary animals, there have been recorded cases of tigers sharing territories and even cooperating in a hunt. While actual cooperation and sharing of a kill is extremely rare, overlapping territories are somewhat common. Within his territory, a male typically has a home range in which he spends most of his time. Neighboring males will often travel the same paths in a section of forest, as long as they do so at different times. A face-to-face encounter will usually lead to aggression. To clearly establish where their territory begins and ends, as well as when they have recently been by, tigers use a series of signals.

Vocalizations

Like many other animals, the tiger utilizes a number of different vocalizations to communicate. The most well known of these is the roar. Only four cats can roar: the tiger, lion, leopard, and jaguar. These cats' throats are constructed in a unique way that allows air passing through a stretchy cartilage to produce a very loud bellowing sound. These large cats have this cartilage in place of the series of small bones that, when vibrating, allow smaller cats to purr. Consequently, a cat can either purr or roar, but not do both. The roar is typically used to establish the tiger's territory. Very often at dawn and dusk, a tiger's roar can be heard up to several miles away, making it an effective tool for long-range communication. The sound will ring through the jungle, letting others know that the resident tiger is around. The roar can also be used to invite adversaries to a fight, or scare them off from beginning one.

Tigers make other sounds as well. Snarls, growls, and hisses are not uncommon. These are typically used as warnings, general mood indicators, or precursors to aggression. A growl, for example, is often used as a sign of general annoyance. Tigresses will often growl at their cubs when they're misbehaving in some way. A "chuff" is a sound tigers make to each other as a greeting. Mothers can be heard chuffing to their young very often to reassure them or to call to them. A chuff sounds like vibrating air passing through the animal's lips. Each tiger's roar, growl, and chuff is unique, and other tigers can recognize the identity of its originator from quite some distance.

Physical markings

While vocalizations can be heard over great distances, they do not leave any permanent remains. So tigers also use a number of physical markings to identify their presence. Claw marks in trees, scraping up the ground, and defecating serve to alert others that a tiger has passed by. One of the most useful marks a tiger employs is the scent mark. Just like the domestic cat, tigers will spray their urine on anything they consider their territory. This scent is full of information for roving tigers. The tiger will check out the smell by engaging in what is known as "flehmen" behavior. The tiger approaches the marked object, wrinkles its nose and opens its mouth wide. It is actually a very comical looking display, but it enables the tiger to draw more of the smell into its mouth to reach the Jacobson's organ. This direct link to the tiger's brain allows it to determine the sex, approximate age, and, if previously encountered, the individual identity of the scent's creator. Female tigers will also disclose their state of sexual receptivity through the hormone levels in their scent mark. This is a very useful tool, as it allows tigers who may overlap territories to see where their neighbors have been. They can also determine, through the relative freshness of the scent,

how long it has been since the other tiger has passed through. By keeping track of the appropriate marks, tigers can avoid bumping into each other, which invariably leads to some type of aggression. While tigers will not hesitate to fight among themselves when necessary, they would rather conserve their energy for hunting their prey.

A Bengal tiger marks a tree in its territory. Tigers learn the age and sex of other tigers in the area by smelling the scents these neighbors have left on marked objects.

The hunt

In many ways, the tiger is the perfect predator. Every part of its body is designed for locating, capturing, and killing its prey. It has a powerfully constructed skull and jaw to absorb the impact of an attack. Special muscles around the lower jaw allow it to exert great pressure and bite through vertebrae, or clamp the throat to strangle. Long, sharp canines are used to pierce the flesh and get a good hold of the prey. The tiger's cheek teeth meet in the back like the blades of a scissor to slice through tough meat and tendons. A muscular torso and strong legs allow it to sneak stealthily along the ground with a smooth gliding motion. Its paws are covered with soft pads that are very sensitive and allow the cat to carefully maneuver its way through the terrain without making any noise.

Its orange coloration and dark striped pattern may seem to stand out boldly in a zoo setting, but in the jungle it is the perfect camouflage. The stripes serve to break up the shape of the tiger. Most prey animals have the basic shapes of danger hard-wired into their brains and will automatically run from anything shaped like a cat or a large bird of prey. By breaking up the basic predator outline, the prey becomes confused. In addition, the stripes mimic the shadows cast at dusk by the tall grass. Tigers generally hunt at dawn or dusk, when the landscape is flooded with the rays of the low-lying sun. As the tiger moves through the thick brush, its pattern blends in well with the sun and shadows.

A group of Indian sambar deer wades in water. Tigers prize such large prey because the meat will keep the hunters fed for several days.

Unlike most felines, the tiger is comfortable in water and will spend part of its day splashing around in streams or watering holes.

Typically, a tiger will go after anything it can catch. However, it prefers the big kills, such as deer, as these will keep it fed for days. Of course, it does have its favorites. One of the tiger's most common prey is the sambar, the largest of the Indian deer. A sambar stands five feet at the shoulder and can weigh over 650 pounds. Another favorite of the tiger is a small deer known as the chital, or spotted beauty. Some tigers seem to have a real taste for chital, even being observed to ignore other prey when one is nearby. Tigers will also commonly go after other types of hoofstock such as hog deer, muntjacs, nilgai, and even gaur and wild buffalo.

During the day, the tiger spends most of its time lounging around, sleeping or splashing around in a body of water. Tigers are one of the only cats that actually enjoy being in the water. Once dusk arrives, if it is hungry, it will begin to survey the local watering holes. It must move in quietly because if even one prey animal is alerted to the tiger's presence, it will send out an alarm call, scaring off every animal in earshot.

Sometimes the tiger will simply lie in wait by a waterhole or a well-traveled path. This gives the tiger the advantage of conserving energy, and allows the prey to get very close to the tiger before it must pounce. However, the disadvantage is that it may wait all day and night without encountering a suitable meal. More often the tiger will travel through its territory looking for something to eat. Once the desired prey is spotted, the tiger will begin to follow it. It will use its well-designed body and well-honed skills to remain absolutely silent and unseen. Once the tiger gets as close as it can, it will lie still, pulling its legs in underneath it. Its body tenses, preparing to pounce. In the final moment, it will bob its head up and down, gauging the distance one final time, and then explode with full force at its prey. The tiger is not capable of sustained speed, so it must hit its mark on the first try or risk losing its meal.

The tiger has a few methods of killing depending on the size and type of prey. Whenever possible, it prefers to grab the prey from the back of the neck. In this way, it can use its powerful jaws to crush the vertebrae, severing the spinal cord and killing its victim almost instantly. When this neck grip is not possible, the tiger will go for the underside of the throat, hoping to sever the jugular with its sharp teeth, or hang on long enough to suffocate it. On some occasions (usually when attacking very large or dangerous prey), the tiger will first attempt to disable its prey by slashing out with its claws. It will attempt to cut a hamstring or slash other vital areas, bringing the prey down and allowing for a quick blow to the neck.

Once it has made its kill, the tiger will use its sharp teeth and claws to tear open the carcass and begin eating. An adult tiger can eat as much as sixty pounds of meat in one sitting. If there is meat left over, it will stay nearby to keep an eye on its kill and protect it from scavengers. The tiger will come back several nights in a row to feed on the same carcass.

Tigers and humans

The word *tiger* was coined by the Romans. They named it after the swift and strong Tigris River of Mesopotamia. However, the Romans did not see their first tiger until about 50 B.C. Other civilizations had a much earlier and richer involvement with the tiger. The earliest evidence of human interaction with the tiger exists on seals from the Indus valley civilizations of Harappa and Mohenjodaro (now Pakistan). These seals were worn as amulets about five thousand years ago. There are records of tiger hunts from three thousand years ago, in the court of Egyptian pharaoh Amenhotep III. The first European to have seen a tiger was probably Alexander the Great. After invading Persia in 330 B.C., he hunted them. Not surprisingly, tigers also figure prominently in the Hindu religion. The Hindu goddess Durga, around whom a nine-day festival is celebrated, is usually depicted riding a tiger. Even today, many Indian truckers have a picture of Durga and her tiger mount painted on their trucks, apparently for luck on the road.

A mighty Bengal tiger walks through the surf. Ever since humans first encountered the tiger, they have been in awe of the creature's beauty and strength.

The tiger in folk legends

Of course, being an animal that has lived in close proximity to Asian tribal cultures, the tiger has figured prominently in many of their folk legends. There are stories about both good and evil tigers influencing the survival and development of many ethnic groups. For example, the Minangkabau people of Sumatra view most tigers as "good." However, they believe every now and then a tiger will be possessed by a "bad" spirit and wander into human territory to become a potential man-eater. When this happens, a special tiger shaman is called in to capture the animal. The shaman baits a trap with meat, and then sits by it, for days if necessary, playing ritualistic tunes that have been passed down from generation to generation. Eventually the corrupted tiger is caught, and then speared to death. Another very common belief in southern Asia is the story of the weretiger. Much like the European werewolf, the weretiger is a man who has been possessed by a tiger spirit. The individual is believed to transform into a tiger and go out hunting humans. Many tribal people have been put to death when accused of such a crime.

A bad reputation

Unfortunately, because of its predatory nature, the tiger has often received a very bad reputation. Europeans especially, though having profound respect for the African lion, seemed contemptuous of the tiger. Tigers were often described as treacherous and bloodthirsty creatures. When Europeans first swarmed through India they engaged in the shikar, or tiger hunt, as a way of demonstrating their mastery of the savage lands of Asia.

Over the last century, many thousands of tigers have been exterminated as pests. Fortunately for the tiger, American field biologist George Schaller helped to give the tiger a better image. In 1964 he began studies of the tiger in the Kanha National Park in India. He traveled on foot, studying their social behavior and getting very close to the animals. Through his research, he was able to show the world that tigers are not the mindless killing machines they have been made out to be. By sharing their complex and often affectionate cub-rearing practices, Schaller was able to raise the public's opinion of the tiger and consequently inspire some people to begin preserving it in its natural habitat. Of course, saving the tiger will be a long and arduous process, and for every George Schaller, there are a thousand people who want the tiger killed, either to protect themselves and their livestock, or to cash in on the profitable business of tiger poaching and deforestation.

2

Habitat Loss

PERHAPS THE LARGEST single problem affecting all wildlife today is finding room to live. The tiger, for example, once spread throughout most of the forested regions of Asia. According to John Seidensticker, curator of mammals at the National Zoo in Washington, D.C., and chairman of the Save the Tiger Fund, all a tiger needs to survive is shelter, water, and prey. These seem like simple requirements, but they become more difficult to find with each passing year. The earth has a finite amount of resources. It is capable of sustaining only a specific amount of life, referred to as its "carrying capacity." As the population of one species increases, somewhere the population of another must decrease. The human race has grown steadily over the last few hundred millennia, but during the last few centuries, it has skyrocketed to outrageous proportions. Humanity's strong drive to survive and reproduce has hurried the extinction and endangerment of countless plants and animals.

According to population trend researchers, this increase in humankind can be attributed primarily to improved technology and medical treatment. Humans can produce crops and raise livestock faster than ever before. People live longer lives than ever thought possible. Not only are humans living almost three times as long, but they are continuing to reproduce well into these later years, and the infant mortality rate has dropped to a mere fraction of what it used to be.

The lush, green jungle environment that is home to some tiger species is being lost to settlement and the timber industry.

Humans have also found the ability to colonize every conceivable type of terrain, from mountains to deserts. The bulk of all this expansion has occurred in the underdeveloped nations of southeast Asia, where most of the wild lands, and most of the world's tigers, remain.

To support this expanded population, the earth is being taxed very heavily in the form of mining, fishing, agriculture, and deforestation. Rivers are continually dammed and diverted, and swamps are drained. Tropical forests, where the tiger is primarily found, once encompassed 1.66 million square miles in southeast Asia. More than half of these forests have already been destroyed: cleared to make room for agriculture and provide grazing areas for cattle, as well as fuel and building materials for the millions of local people who inhabit the area. Still more lumber is collected for commercial export to developed countries. As humans build their own houses and enrich their own lives, they continue to chip away at the homes and livelihood of the world's tiger population.

Regional overviews

Each area of the world struggles with its own individual problems concerning the preservation of wild habitats. For example, the Amur tiger, often referred to as the Siberian tiger despite the fact that its range does not extend into Siberia, came very close to extinction around the turn of the century when settlers began to populate the area. In the 1930s it was estimated that only 20 to 30 were left in the wild. Due to the strict policing efforts of the Soviet Union during most of this century, today the numbers are back up to between 350 and 400 tigers. Measuring 625 square miles, the Sikhote-Alin preserve in the heart of the Amur tiger's range has been one of the largest tracts of undisturbed habitat for tigers. However, the new Russian government is undergoing severe financial difficulty and can no longer afford to divert enough funds to protect this region. It has even begun selling off logging rights in the area to Asian and Western companies to raise capital.

One of the estimated five to six hundred Sumatran tigers thought to exist in the wild. Even though numbers of some tiger populations may be increasing, researchers fear there are not enough to ensure the species' survival.

Under the rule of Mao Zedong, the South China tiger was hunted as a pest. It was nearly exterminated; today, researchers estimate there may be as few as twenty to thirty left. These are scattered between four disconnected sec-

tions of forest, and many scientists feel there are not enough left to bounce back to a viable population.

Until recently, it was thought that the Sumatran tiger was also on its way out. However, recent research employing modern techniques such as camera traps that are triggered by passing animals, conducted by Ron Tilson of the Minnesota Zoo, has shown that an estimated thirty-six tigers live in one park that was thought to be virtually empty of tigers. The newest estimates in Sumatra still put the population count at somewhere between five and six hundred.

Because Thailand is a difficult area to study, for both political and environmental reasons, there are no completely accurate tallies of the number of tigers left there. However, a recent expedition conducted by Wildlife Conservation Society researcher Alan Rabinowitz discovered that, despite vast expanses of pristine forest, there were very few, if any, tigers. Thailand's government officially reports the population as ranging between 250 and 600.

The world takes notice

The International Union for the Conservation of Nature (IUCN) is an international organization that sponsors research and discussion of the endangered status of the world's plant and animal populations. The findings of its individual research programs are widely accepted by the governments of the world as the most accurate and up-to-date information. Each year the IUCN updates its "Red List" which identifies the most critically endangered species. While this group has no authority to create any laws regarding protection, its recommendations are acted upon by most of the world's governments in the form of local laws concerning the use of wild lands, poaching, and trade in animal products. In 1969 the IUCN met in New Delhi, bringing together conservationists from all around the world to discuss the endangerment of the tiger population. It identified two major causes for the drastic decrease in wild tigers. One was that humans have increased accessibility to tiger habitats. Until the last few decades, most

The dense, foreboding jungle landscapes that once protected tigers like this Indo-Chinese adult are steadily being overcome by humans in need of space and the forest's resources.

tigers lived deep in the heart of impenetrable forests, isolated from humans. No roads or navigable waterways existed, and any person adventurous enough to blaze their own path was very likely to contract malaria from the incredible number of mosquitoes. During the latter half of the twentieth century, however, technology in the form of massive clear-cutting machinery and all-terrain vehicles opened up direct access routes to the heart of many of Asia's densest jungles. The development of the chemical DDT helped to wipe out the mosquitoes and any real threat of malaria. The tiger was no longer hidden, and humans began to move into its domain.

The second factor had to do with increased wealth in Asian nations during the 1950s and 1960s. As these nations entered the world market, a select number of their citizens discovered new wealth and a whole new standard of living. Although the vast majority of Asian citizens were still stricken with poverty, the increased wealth of the upper classes brought an increased demand for tiger furs, bones (used for medicinal purposes), and trophies. More people owned firearms, which made the average hunter a much more efficient killing machine. A single person could now take down as many tigers in a week as their ancestors had in a year. The death toll finally climbed high enough that the IUCN placed the tiger on its Red List, declaring it an officially endangered species. It was now up to the individual governments of the world to enact and enforce real laws to safeguard the tiger.

Anatomy of a preserve

Designating areas for protection is an important first step in habitat preservation. However, true success can only be achieved if the preserves are properly planned and managed. The IUCN Cat Specialist Group recognized three factors in stabilizing the tiger's habitat. The first was creating multispecies and specialized wildlife refuges and providing effective protection for existing preserves. These would serve as the core areas in which tigers, and other wildlife, could live unmolested. The second factor was to identify and protect territories that serve as forested corridors between preserves, allowing for the continual movement of tigers and their prey. Lastly, assistance had to be provided to ethnic groups to help preserve cultural traditions and native lifestyles. Valmik Thapar pointed out that any real progress in protecting habitat will rely on the cooperation of the local Asian people. They hold the key to the tiger's survival, as well as the ammunition for its destruction.

The IUCN has made recommendations about how to achieve these goals. For example, it suggests that no government be allowed to make decisions about the development of any lands containing tiger populations without the inclusion of an IUCN (or other recognized international group) representative. This ensures that the policies about habitat preservation and conservation will be more uniform and less influenced by individual financial gain. It also recommends the stimulation of technological research to produce fast-growth trees and better land-use management, which would allow countries to gain more productivity from smaller areas of land. Ecotourism should also be a strong component of raising funds and public awareness, and bringing to light the importance of the tiger in the eyes of the local people. The more tourists that come to see a given preserve, the more money they bring into the area, and consequently, the more likely the locals will want to keep the preserve around. One of the primary ideas is to create and refine a model program of multifaceted sustainable forest use, which should be created in an area complete with native villages. The Cat Specialist Group believes that the knowledge it gains from studying and manipulating the model preserve can be used to establish a large chain of new preserves.

There has been much debate between governments and conservation groups as to what makes a suitable preserve. When targeting an area for protection, it is not usually possible to block it off completely from all human impact. The human population surge in most of Asia means that nearly all tiger habitats are in close proximity to people. To make habitat protection a realistic possibility, most conservationists recognize a need for a central protection area surrounded by rings of buffer zones, in which gradually increasing human activity would be permitted. In this way, the tigers in the core area would be completely undisturbed and free to live and breed normally. The buffer zones would give the tigers the option of moving out into other areas if necessary, and at the same time provide local humans with some of the forest resources they need.

Manageable zoning

The Hornocker Institute, an independent tiger habitat research group, has developed an outline for manageable zoning, which explains the proposed functions of each zone. Originally developed for the Amur tiger, the plan seems applicable to tiger habitat preservation throughout Asia.

Zone one would be the central core of the preserve and would provide the highest level of protection. In this area, protection of tigers would take precedence over all else. No logging or hunting would be permitted, and the area would remain 100 percent forested (except for natural openings).

In zone two, tiger conservation would be one of the most important components in all land-use planning, but some controlled use of the land would be acceptable. This area would maintain 90 percent of its forest cover. Only selective cutting would be allowed; all roads developed during logging would be sealed after the operation ends; and hunting of animals such as deer and boar would be regulated to insure a high level of prey availability for the tigers.

Land use, hunting, and biological corridors

Zone three would consist of areas where tigers are found and efforts are made to manage them, but also where other land uses can have high priority. Here, forests should make up at least 70 percent of the land. Road closures would occur whenever possible, and game hunting would be monitored to some degree. Any decisions about land use in these areas should involve an environmental impact assessment for the tiger population.

In zone four, tigers would be tolerated, should they wander out of the inner zones, but no official management activities would be specified, besides standard national and local laws concerning hunting and land use. Anything past zone four would be deemed unacceptable for tiger habitation. Tigers found to regularly venture into these regions would be frightened away or captured and relocated to another area.

In addition to organizing a system of buffer zones for individual preserves, there would need to be areas protected as forested highways or biological corridors between preserves. Without these corridors, the tiger populations would be isolated. Young males would not have the ability to safely wander off in search of new territory. Since a tiger will always choose the path with the most cover, if forested bridges between preserves were supplied, the tiger would move through them, rather than venturing out in another direction, possibly into a village or farming community where it would be shot.

Genetics

Another important impact of the biological corridors would be to prevent inbreeding. Even if an area is large enough to house all the tigers in the area, they cannot survive isolation. If tigers do not have access to other distinct populations, they will inbreed with one another. From a biological standpoint, this would be very unhealthy. The process of evolution allows for changing environments. A species must continually reinvent itself to survive in the face of these changes. The way it does this is through "survival of the fittest." When a random change, or mutation, occurs that proves beneficial to the animal's survival, that animal lives longer and produces more offspring (which carry the same genetic features). These new animals, which are better adapted to survival in the new environment, must be able to mix their genes into other populations if survival of the species as a whole is to occur.

Depending on who you ask, biologists say that a connected population of thirty to five hundred tigers is necessary to maintain a healthy and genetically diverse tiger

A Bengal tiger wades in the waters of India's Ranthambhore National Park. Such preserves help keep people out of tiger habitats, but naturalists believe more needs to be done so that these animals are not forced to remain in isolated communities.

A Sumatran tigress and her cub in a zoo. By breeding tigers in captivity, scientists hope that they can control gene pools and ensure that those released back into the wild will be strong enough to survive.

population. With anything less, they may survive, but they will be at a serious evolutionary disadvantage. Unfortunately, these numbers don't exist in many areas. Scientists have identified three methods of mixing up the gene pool, but none of them is completely plausible yet.

One suggestion involves the introduction of captive-bred cubs from zoos and breeding programs. This method would allow scientists to accurately control which genes are going where. However, it is expensive and time-consuming, and there is no guarantee that the cubs would survive in the wild. Translocation of tigers from one area in the wild to another is another possibility. Adult tigers could be captured and relocated hundreds of miles away. This method is more popular with certain groups, as it does not involve keeping any tigers in captivity. Some researchers point out, though, that this method could lead to aggression problems between tigers, resulting from the need to reestablish their territories. The final method would involve artificially inseminating wild female tigers with genetic material from other areas. This is a relatively new science and is far from being perfected or cost effective. Future research may make this option the most viable.

Humans vs. tigers

Perhaps the biggest obstacle to habitat preservation is the resistance it faces from local inhabitants of the protected areas. The people that live in or near the preserves are often denied access to local development such as new roads, irrigation systems, or urbanization. These things are not permitted near the preserves, which causes hardship and resentment. The governments of tiger countries (especially India) are trying to alleviate the problem by relocating the people to other areas.

There are a number of large problems that occur when locals live in close proximity to tiger preserves. Many Asian villagers survive by breeding livestock. There are over 1 billion head of cattle in India alone. All these animals must eat, so their owners take them to graze inside the preserve boundaries, as they have grazed the borderlands into near deserts. This grazing takes away food from the local deer population, which serves as prey for the tiger.

Villagers also hunt wild deer and boar for food. With the increased human population, the advent of modern firearms, and the opportunities for commercial marketing of meat, the natural prey of the tiger is disappearing at an unbelievable rate. According to George Schaller of the Wildlife Conservation Society, even in areas like Indochina where the forest itself remains almost completely intact, there is nothing left within to feed the tigers. The local people have hunted the wild hoofstock almost to extinction.

Another problem involves the taking of wood as fuel and building materials. Typically, people think of large corporations as being responsible for clear-cutting forests. In Asia, however, the human population is so large that the impact of individual villages collecting firewood and building materials is immense. Deforestation occurs on epic scales wherever humans are found.

As the numbers of tigers within preserves increases, the number of encounters between humans and tigers inevitably rises as well. "Man-eating" tigers have long been a problem in certain areas of India. The Sundarbans is a marshy area in India with one of the world's highest populations of wild tiger. For some reason, this area has been plagued with more than its share of human fatalities from tiger attacks. Until recently, though, the Sundarbans was the exception. Today, as the tiger population begins to recover and human numbers increase, tiger attacks are occurring in many areas. And many locals are very angry that the government protects these killer tigers. Peter Jackson, chairman of IUCN's Cat Specialist Group, recalls the angry cry of villagers as they set out to hunt down a tiger that had killed one of their people: "You don't care about us. If we kill a tiger, we go to prison, but if a tiger kills one of us, we are just dogs." In an effort to placate the local people, the government of India hunts down and traps, or kills, any tigers that are deemed "repeat offenders." It also provides monetary compensation for livestock that has been killed (about $154), as well as to the families of people who have been killed (about $384). However, when people take matters into their own hands, they can be fined up to $400 and spend six months in jail.

Finding a solution

All of these problems are major stumbling blocks in the preservation of tigers and their habitat. According to

Valmik Thapar, a naturalist and filmmaker who has studied tigers for more than twenty-five years, "Villagers must be involved in these parks, must be made to feel a part of these necessary changes, not their helpless victims. The future of Indian wildlife ultimately rests with the villages that surround them." This idea would seem to apply to habitat preservation worldwide. He has proposed numerous ideas for incentives for local people to get involved with conservation. The idea, says Thapar, is to provide such excellent incentives that people actually look forward to having their areas made into protected regions. When an area becomes a preserve, the locals can benefit by obtaining government subsidies for relocation, better housing, jobs at the preserve, and even a share of the money brought in by ecotourists.

Of course, not everyone is so optimistic. Billy Singh, one of India's most outspoken tiger conservationists, sees these as long-term goals, but in the short term he believes tigers and people simply need to be kept apart. He has argued to have high electric fences constructed around Dudhwa National Park and to ban any agriculture for a five-mile radius around the park. According to Singh, the choice between leaving the land for tigers or people is clear: "Tigers *need* unmolested forest in which to multiply. People can breed anywhere."

Project Tiger

When it comes to a commitment to tiger preservation, no nation can surpass India. It has blazed ahead to become the world leader in tiger protection. In 1972 the Indian government launched a task force to investigate the status of the Bengal tiger population. It found that only 1,980 tigers were left in India, and 420 in the nations of Nepal, Bhutan, and Bangladesh.

Alarmed by these numbers, then prime minister Indira Gandhi declared the tiger India's national symbol and proclaimed her commitment to save the species. She was a driving force behind the creation of Project Tiger, a program that has since been recognized as an amazingly effective conservation effort for such a young nation with so many other pressing economic and social issues. No other country, before or since, has mounted as serious an effort to preserve such a powerful and potentially destructive predator.

Project Tiger had two main objectives when it began: to ensure the maintenance of a viable population of tigers and to preserve, for all time, areas of biological importance, or intact forest ecosystems, as a national heritage for the benefit, education, and enjoyment of the people. The program began by designating and setting aside nine key areas as special tiger preserves. Within these preserves, hunting, mining, removal of wood or other materials for fuel, cattle grazing, and commercial development were prohibited.

Despite other pressing affairs of state, Indira Gandhi pledged her support to saving India's tiger populations during her term as prime minister.

This was a very tall order, as many local people were located in or near the preserves, and they depended on its resources for their livelihood. In addition, India stood to lose a lot of money by prohibiting commercial development.

Kailash Sankhala was appointed the first director of Project Tiger, and his initial goal was to convince the local state governments to give up their profitable logging businesses within the newly protected areas. To achieve this, the central Indian government provided financial incentives in the form of subsidies, or monetary support, for companies discontinuing these practices. Sankhala was fairly successful in stopping the practice.

The next big obstacle was to educate the local people. Programs were initiated to help people understand the importance of tiger preservation, but this was not enough. Project Tiger relocated entire villages outside the preserves. It prepared new fields for the translocated villagers to farm and built medical clinics, schools, and temples. Some of the villagers were very happy about this, since tigers were killing their livestock and the logging industry had shut down, leaving many people without work. Others, however, felt uprooted from the traditional homes of their ancestors, and resisted the move. In the end, all villages inside the preserves were moved, and the local people were assisted in making a new life.

Free of the pressures of clear-cutting and massive numbers of livestock, much of the vegetation in the preserves regenerated. In 1979 a census reported three thousand tigers in India. Part of this increase was probably due to improved census-taking methods. In 1989 there were reportedly four thousand tigers. The number of Project Tiger preserves at that time had risen to seventeen.

A tragic setback

The program was doing very well, until an unfortunate setback. In 1984 Indira Gandhi was assassinated. As Gandhi was one of the driving forces behind Project Tiger, her death left it without one of its strongest proponents. The organization of India's central government fell into turmoil. As political power began to move away from New Delhi and over to the local politicians in individual states, it became more difficult to enforce nationwide tiger protection laws. In addition, India's caste system, which ranks people according to their social standing, began to break down. More poor citizens were able to vote and many of them voted against tiger protection, as they saw the tiger as a serious threat to themselves and their livestock. They also saw its prey as a source of food and the land as a source of fuel. These factors caused a major setback in the progress of Project Tiger. However, the program did continue and has managed to not only sustain the improvements it made but also, in the 1990s, to expand them. Today there are twenty-three Project Tiger preserves, and more than thirty-six hundred people are permanently employed by them. These preserves cover over thirty thousand square kilometers and house about one-third of all India's wild tigers (about thirteen hundred). All together India has over thirty-seven hundred tigers, more than half of the world's tiger population.

3

The Hunt

FOR MILLENNIA, THE tiger existed at the very top of the food chain, hunting to survive. As humans began to appear in its habitat, however, the tiger suddenly became the hunted. For centuries now humankind has occupied the top position on the food chain. The difference between humans hunting tigers and tigers hunting their prey, however, is that tigers hunt only to survive, while people hunt for a variety of reasons. Humans, as a species, have engaged in the systematic eradication of the tiger for many generations. The tiger is hunted for sport, food, furs, medicines, and self-preservation.

Sport

The tradition of hunting tigers for sport goes back a very long time. Ancient civilizations in Asia, ranging from China to Bali, considered it a way of testing one's strength and virility. As the years went by, human numbers increased, and consequently, so did the tiger kills. Official records and journals provide historians with countless examples of not only single tiger hunts, but mass slaughter as well. For example, between 1821 and 1828, one small village in India killed over one thousand tigers in ritualistic hunts. British officer William Rice shot 93 Indian tigers while on safari between 1850 and 1854. A man named Gordon Cumming killed 173 in 1863. One member of the Bengal civil service reportedly killed 400 during his twenty-five-year tenure.

The hunting of tigers for sport became especially fashionable at the turn of the century. Wealthy nobles from Europe would pay large sums of money to go on real tiger hunts. Sometimes they would pay for private safaris led by locals. Very often these nobles were the guests of maharajas, or Indian royalty, who would entertain the Europeans by taking them out to engage in this bloody sport. Using skilled trackers and modern firearms, they could "bag" an extraordinary number of tigers. The maharaja of Nepal, for example, entertained King George V during his stay in 1911 by shooting 39 tigers in eleven days. The record, though, is thought to be held by the maharaja of Surguja who claimed to have killed 1,150 tigers during his lifetime.

Of course, tigers were also hunted for reasons other than sport. Historians have revealed that during the nineteenth century, Russian soldiers moving eastward toward Turkey were reported to have shot thousands of tigers during training exercises. When they reached the Caspian Sea, they

A nineteenth-century photograph of Indian villagers carrying a slain tiger. For centuries these animals have been hunted either for sport or because they were thought dangerous to human settlements.

were instructed to eradicate the tigers they found to clear the way for settlers. They did a very efficient job: Today the Caspian tiger is completely extinct. Until very recently, in China large bounties were paid by the government to destroy tigers as pests. According to Chinese scientists Lou Houji and Sheng Helin, about three thousand tigers were killed during a thirty-year period earlier this century. In fact, tigers had no official protection in China until 1977. Today a mere handful are left.

The traditional hunt

In years past, the tiger hunt was carried out in a very ritualized fashion. A young buffalo or goat was staked out while the hunters waited patiently in a nearby tree. They would remain completely silent until they spotted the tiger just below them. Then, they would shoot, either killing it instantly or wounding it and following the trail of blood into the forest, where they would finish it off. Wealthier hunters would hire elephants and "beaters" to flush the tiger out from its cover and corral it toward the mounted hunter, who would then shoot it from his protected vantage. These same methods were used by local people from Russia, throughout China, Nepal, India, Sumatra, Bali, and anywhere else the tiger was found. These cats were most often hunted either as food or pests. With the great amount of skill, courage, and time required, tiger hunts were difficult and kills were kept low enough to allow the species as a whole to survive.

Opening the gateway

Things changed drastically though during the middle of the twentieth century. The end of World War II may well have marked the beginning of the end for the tiger. Forests throughout British-controlled India were clear-cut to provide resources for the Allies' war effort; all-terrain vehicles were produced, providing ready access to previously hidden terrain; and firearms became more sophisticated and easily available. Then, in 1947, India gained its independence and much of the nobles' pristine land was taken over

by local people. These new guns and jeeps became available to a much larger percentage of the population. Excited by their newfound freedom and opportunity, many Indian people ranged through the forest, shooting anything they came across. Rich tourists also flooded the shores of the "new" India, setting their sights on bagging a tiger.

As locals moved into the forest, incidences of "maneaters" increased and people went on killing sprees through the forests, armed with their new weaponry. All this resulted in a mass slaughter of the species as a whole. At the turn of the century, there were reportedly forty thousand Bengal tigers in the world. By 1969, Kailash Sankhala of the Indian Forest Service claimed that number was down to less than twenty-five hundred.

In the late nineteenth and early twentieth centuries, Europeans often went on safari in India to hunt tigers. Indian natives were eager to assist on these expeditions because of the wealth the tourists brought to local communities.

Beginning of protection

In the late 1960s, people began to take notice of the tiger's downward population trends. Many conservation groups were alarmed by reports that claimed that from

*Tiger skins adorn the
floor of a maharaja's
palace. Such trophy
hunting was legal in
India until the 1960s.*

1966 to 1969, when hunting was still legal in India, 480 tigers were officially recorded shot. The figure was misleadingly low, considering the Indian Ministry of Foreign Trade reported exports of raw tiger and leopard skins for the same years at 11,290 kilograms. This would represent approximately 2,260 tigers and/or leopards. Tigers were much more popular game, but if even half of these were tiger skins, it is clear that the number of actual tiger kills is far greater than reflected by national records.

As a result of this data, the IUCN decided to add the Bengal tiger to their Red List of endangered species. The other tiger subspecies were already listed as endangered. At this time a complete halt, or moratorium, on all Bengal tiger hunting was put in place until further studies could be conducted to determine if Sankhala's estimate of twenty-five hundred tigers was accurate. By 1971 a complete ban was put in effect in all parts of India despite protests from hunters and foresters. In 1972 the new official census reported a mere eighteen hundred tigers in India.

To combat endangerment of all species, including the tiger, in 1975 the Convention on International Trade in Endangered Species (CITES) was created to link the governments of the world in a global system of trade control. Like most UN treaties and conventions, CITES cannot impose international sanctions or penalties, and no governments are required to join on as signatories, or members. They must voluntarily choose to join the convention. The incentive to joining and abiding by the rulings, however, comes in the form of political pressure. Joining CITES was seen, in the international community, as the correct thing to do. Today there are 132 signatory nations.

CITES categorizes species into one of three groups that determines how they or their by-products may be traded across national borders: Appendix I (no commercial trade allowed), Appendix II (controlled trade only), or Appendix III (monitored trade). The appendix an animal ends up in depends on the current status of its world population, which is often a hot topic for debate at the annual CITES conferences. Typically, a research or conservation group will propose that a particular species be moved up or down the appendixes. The board will then review the current population trend research, listen to reports from supporters and detractors of the move, and then make a decision. Once an animal is placed on Appendix I, all the signatories agree to halt all import and export of live or dead specimens, as well as products made from the animal. In 1976, CITES placed the tiger on Appendix I.

Regulations and sanctions

International wildlife trade is monitored by a number of groups such as TRAFFIC, a branch of the World Wildlife Fund responsible for keeping tabs on the imports and exports of animals and animal products all across the world. Failure to observe the CITES regulations results in the disapproval of other nations, which can affect a country's ability to function in the world market. For example, in 1989, the Environmental Investigation Agency of London provided evidence, based on undercover investigative research and sting operations, that Taiwan was continuing to deal in the trade of tiger parts for medicinal purposes. It called for action to be taken, but nothing was really done. In March 1993, eighty-six organizations led by Earth Island Institute and England's Tiger Trust petitioned the CITES board to recommend action against Taiwan and China for failing to curb their illegal trade. The committee gave them six months to stop. In September 1993, the board reconvened and decided that sufficient changes had not been made and threatened sanctions.

This caused China to move much more quickly. By 1994, it stated that it had assigned forty thousand people to enforce its trade laws. The government also said it had shut down factories and confiscated and burned one thousand pounds of tiger bones. It even began to investigate the possibilities of captive breeding programs to supply the tiger products in demand.

Taiwan's efforts were far less substantial. It claimed to be setting up government agencies to regulate the trade, but according to Earth Island Institute, the agency never really materialized. In April 1994, President Bill Clinton

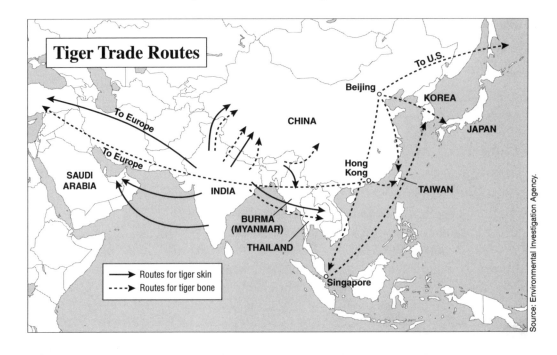

made an unprecedented move by enacting an obscure stipulation of the U.S. Fisherman's Protective Act, which authorized the United States to impose sanctions on any nation determined to be engaging in the willful endangerment of any IUCN Red List species. The U.S. government banned all imports of legal animal products (mostly lizard and snake skin) from Taiwan. This trade typically brings in $25 million a year for Taiwan. This didn't put much of a dent in the overall annual trade between Taiwan and America, which typically amounts to one thousand times that amount. As a symbolic gesture, on the other hand, it carried a lot of weight by setting a precedent for future sanctions and penalties against any nation that chose to ignore CITES regulations. Taiwan responded by cracking down on its tiger trade industry immediately. In July 1995, the United States was satisfied with the changes reported by the Environmental Investigation Agency and lifted the sanctions.

Kaziranga

Controlling a trade that stems from the market demands of a human population as enormous as that of Asia is no easy task, and it will take years to get it completely under control. There are, however, some areas where the battle is already being won. The Kaziranga National Park in east India is well known for its hard-line attitude toward poachers. According to Bhupen Talukdar, a range officer, "Only God can keep people from killing tigers in other parks. Here *we* do it." Talukdar has 400 guards working for him and 120 permanent outposts on the property. At the sound of a shot, it takes only minutes for armed guards to descend on the area of intrusion. These guards are very serious about protecting the park. In the past four years, twenty poachers have been killed trying to make off with rhino horns or tiger bones. Some guards have lost their lives as well. These underpaid and overworked rangers at places like Kaziranga are the grassroots foundation of wildlife conservation. Peter Jackson summed it up well at a press conference in 1995 when he said, "The tiger will virtually be extinct in the wild by 1999, unless India, and other range states declare open war on poachers and illegal traders, and throw all the resources required into the battle."

Crash in the late 1980s

With the advent of CITES, various conservation projects, and an enormous worldwide interest in saving the tiger, the planet's tiger population began to stabilize, and in some localized preserves in Siberia, India, Sumatra, and Nepal, even increase. The future began to look good for the first time in a century. In fact, B. R. Koppikar, a former director of Project Tiger, was even quoted in 1980 as saying, "You can say that there is now no danger of extinction of the tiger in India." These strong words turned out to be overly optimistic.

During the late 1980s, a number of tiger preserves throughout Asia—especially in India and Russia—began to notice a resurgence in poaching. Since the trade of furs and skins had virtually ended, conservationists were at a loss to understand what was happening.

Ranthambhore National Park in India was known as one of the world's greatest conservation success stories. Its tigers had been constantly threatened by poachers and the loss of their prey to local people. Through a number of government-sponsored initiatives, Ranthambhore managed to save its tigers from near extinction. Between 1969 and 1990, the population went from fourteen individuals to forty. It became one of the most well known spots for ecotourism since its tigers could always be counted on to make an appearance. In 1992, however, the jewel in the Project Tiger crown reported some startling findings. Several well-recognized tigers had disappeared. An investigation launched by park officials determined that the park's tiger population had fallen from forty-four to fifteen or twenty tigers.

TRAFFIC began a sting operation in the area, which led to the arrest of several bands of poachers in nearby New Delhi's Tibetan refugee quarter. What it found was more

than 400 kilograms of tiger bones (a total of 850 kilograms were found throughout the surrounding areas). The New Delhi bust alone represented some forty tigers. Suddenly it became clear that the bones were being exported to China and several other Eastern nations. These products are especially in demand in China, where a large part of their traditional medicine involves the use of tiger bones and other body parts. Until the 1980s, the Chinese government had routinely slaughtered its tigers and created a large stockpile of the bones it used for this trade. China's tiger population is now virtually extinct. So once these stockpiles were depleted in the late 1980s, China began to import tiger products, increasing the market for poached tigers. Many local Indian villagers were willing to risk jail because they were paid between $100 and $300 for each tiger they killed, which represents an entire year's wages for many Third World citizens. Money is a strong motivator, and difficult to combat. This industry is now seen as one of the primary factors in the decline of the tiger. One startling statistic in an article in *Time* magazine stated that India,

A tiger lounges near a creek in Ranthambhore National Park. Park rangers fight a constant battle to keep poachers away from the preserve's small but growing population of tigers.

which contains 60 percent of the world's tigers, lost a staggering 35 percent of its tigers between 1989 and 1994.

History of the bone trade

Why do the people of the Far East believe that these tiger bones and other body parts can cure disease? It is simply a matter of cultural tradition. Culture, especially in a nation as old as China, can be firmly entrenched in the lives of its citizens much like religion, and any attempt to alter these beliefs is typically met with resistance. Ancient Chinese medical volumes, dating back some two thousand years, state that tiger flesh improves health and vitality, as well as wards off thirty-six types of demon. Tiger fat is believed to cure hemorrhoids, while tiger blood is believed to improve the constitution and willpower. Tiger eyes can clarify vision and stop crying. A tiger's nose placed on the

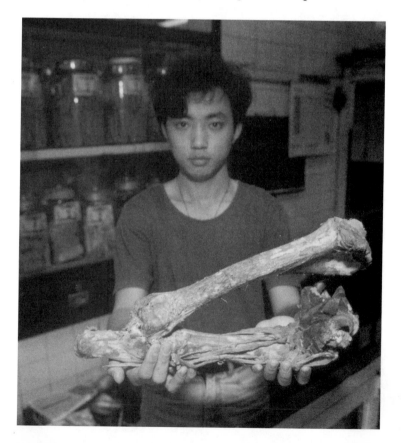

Tiger parts are bought and sold by Asian pharmacists whose customers believe the animal's bones and organs have medicinal powers.

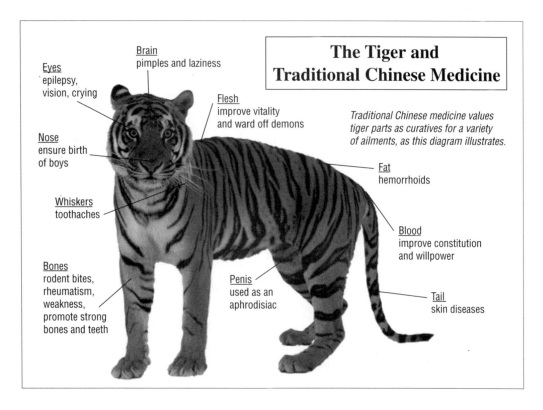

The Tiger and Traditional Chinese Medicine

Brain
pimples and laziness

Eyes
epilepsy, vision, crying

Flesh
improve vitality and ward off demons

Nose
ensure birth of boys

Traditional Chinese medicine values tiger parts as curatives for a variety of ailments, as this diagram illustrates.

Fat
hemorrhoids

Whiskers
toothaches

Blood
improve constitution and willpower

Bones
rodent bites, rheumatism, weakness, promote strong bones and teeth

Penis
used as an aphrodisiac

Tail
skin diseases

roof of a home, theoretically, ensures the birth of boys. Tiger's whiskers can cure a toothache. Claims abound about the properties of tiger bones, ranging from soothing rodent bites to curing a fear of water, as well as promoting strong teeth and bones. The penis is supposed to be a powerful aphrodisiac. The bones of a deer, removed from tiger feces, can be burned to ash and used to cure alcoholism.

While today's modern Chinese texts do ignore most of these claims, they still purport tiger bone as an important ingredient in many types of medicine. Chief among these are curatives for rheumatism, bone marrow disease, and aching muscles and joints. Ground tiger bone is used to make tiger wine, an invigorating tonic. While most doctors in China and Taiwan today do rely on modern medicines to cure illness, many of their patients still prefer to take the more traditional curatives.

In the traditional method used in China, Taiwan, Korea, and other Asian communities, pharmacies and doctors will stock whole bones and shave off small amounts as necessary for individual customers. Prices in Taiwan were quoted at $860–$1,280 U.S. dollars per kilogram in 1992. Any traditional pharmacy that carries herbs and animal parts usually carries tiger bones as well.

These medicines are sold outside of the traditional pharmacies as well. Throughout these same nations, tiger bones are mass-produced in the form of pills, powders, and liquors. During the 1980s, China exported bone to Hong Kong, Malaysia, Singapore, Thailand, and the United States. Hong Kong plays the role of middleman, by taking in raw materials and manufacturing the finished product. It has the highest rate of export for these items in the East.

Understanding the market

The IUCN feels that, "In order to halt commercial tiger poaching, conservationists must understand the organization and dynamics of the tiger bone market." Without truly understanding the market, it will be impossible to curb it. Researchers are trying to determine exactly how common the products are on the shelves; how much of it is real and how much is fake; and what possible substitutes can be provided by Western medicine. Breaking down cultural traditions can be an enormous task. Asian consumers are resistant to the idea of turning their back on traditional medicines they firmly believe have provided relief from chronic pain and illness in their ancestors for centuries. Many Asians also see it as a further breakdown of important cultural values. They feel that these medicines are part of their heritage and they should not be denied them.

Part of the problem with analyzing the tiger bone trade lies in the fact that it is shrouded in secrecy and, in some cases, outright lies. Since this trade is now illegal in most places, no official records are kept, and it is difficult to get accurate statistics about it. One reliable source of information comes from South Korea, where this trade was still legal and monitored until 1993. Customs reports from this country name Indonesia as the major exporter of tiger bone and derivatives. China, Thailand, Malaysia, and India followed close behind. Between 1970 and 1993 in South Korea alone, almost nine thousand kilograms of tiger bone were imported, representing as many as 750 poached tigers.

Other studies have identified the major importers as South Korea, Japan, the United States, Taiwan, and Singapore. China probably has the largest market for this trade, but does little *official* importing. Contrary to these official Chinese records, however, India points to China as the major importer of Bengal tiger bones. All these countries are CITES members and vehemently deny any importing or exporting of these products. However, every investigative team sent into these nations has found tiger bone available in a large percentage of traditional pharmacies.

Another confounding variable to all this is the existence of fake tiger bone products. Not all medicines labeled and sold as containing tiger bone really have any tiger bone in them. It is easy to fool the consumers by substituting the bones of other, less costly, animals. There are actually books in China with photographs that show the difference between real tiger bones and fakes to help consumers distinguish between them. So, not only don't investigators know exactly how much is being manufactured and sold (and to whom), but they don't even know what percentage of it is real.

Understanding a problem is usually half the battle in defeating it. There will always be people who hunt tigers, but the more that is learned about the reasons and methods behind it, the more that can be done to curb it.

4

Research and Captivity

HUMANKIND HAS HAD a fascination with tigers and other cats throughout recorded history. The Romans, for example, displayed tigers in menageries, pageants, and arena combat. *P. tigris* was also popular with the aristocracy of Asia, and there are even records of early Chinese emperors training them for hunting. These same emperors would use the tigers as executioners as well. During more recent times, the tiger has been a staple of circuses and roadside attractions on nearly every continent.

Humankind's interest in tigers has not waned over the centuries, but its attitude toward the species has. No longer does the general public see the tiger as a vicious beast to be tamed or tormented for amusement. Today, people's attitude toward the tiger is generally one of respect and a desire to help lead it back from endangerment. Many humans have taken up the gauntlet and much work is being done to protect habitat and raise the public consciousness about the need for conservation. Sufficient research, however, must be completed to determine the specific needs and way of life of the tiger before any conservation effort can be successful. Researchers need to know accurate details about the tiger's habitat and prey, territory size, breeding and rearing requirements, impact on local people, as well as a host of other things. Today an extensive amount of research is under way, both in the wild and in captivity, to help answer some of these questions.

Chitwan National Park

The Royal Chitwan National Park in Nepal is well known for its groundbreaking scientific research and accurate census-taking methods. A long-term tiger ecology study by American and Nepalese scientists, funded by the Smithsonian Institution of Washington, D.C., combines the most modern research methods with ancient hunting techniques.

This new integrated technique begins with researchers staking out a large piece of meat as bait to lure a tiger in. Once involved in eating its kill, several Nepalese shikaris, or hunters, will hold up two large white sheets to form two walls, as a visual barrier, in the form of a large "V." This will effectively close the tiger in, with an opening on only one side. A marksman, armed with a dart gun, sits in a tree just above the point of the "V." At a given signal, more

Scientists are learning much about the tiger's territorial needs, breeding cycles, and hunting patterns by observing tigers in captivity.

shikaris mounted on elephants crash through the jungle from the open end of the triangle, startling the tiger and sending it rushing off. Faced with visual barriers on both sides, the tiger heads for the only opening it sees, the opening at the point of the "V," right below the marksman. As the tiger rushes straight into range, the marksman fires a tranquilizer. Within minutes the cat collapses in a deep sleep and the researchers will be able to move in.

While it is down, scientists will measure the tiger's body proportions (head to tail, height, girth), examine the body for injuries, and collect any ticks or other parasites. They will measure the length of the canines and remove one incisor (which will later be sectioned to determine the cat's approximate age). The stripe pattern on the cheeks is sketched and later serves as a helpful tool to identify individual tigers. The cat is then weighed and a custom-sized radio collar is placed around its neck. After checking to make sure the transmitter's signal is being picked up by the researcher's equipment, the tiger is injected with an antidote and the team will retreat as it comes around.

On the trail of the tiger

The next day, the tiger will be fully recovered and back to its normal routine. The researcher will mount an elephant and move the antenna until the familiar "ping" in the headphones is heard. Once it is determined which direction the signal is coming from, the researcher draws a line on the map, from that location to the source of the signal. Then the process is repeated in another area. After drawing the second line on the map, the researcher marks the spot where the two lines cross to reveal the location of the tiger. Over a period of weeks, these marks will allow the researcher to determine the cat's territory and favorite hunting grounds.

The radio collar also allows researchers to locate the tiger's prey. After it has finished eating, the team will move in and inspect the carcass. By doing this, they can determine the tiger's preferred prey, the method of killing, and the average amount of food it takes in. Fecal samples are also collected and studied. As a direct result of these studies, the Nepalese government agreed to expand the protected borders of Chitwan National Park. It was determined that without this expansion the park would be too small for long-term conservation success. These groundbreaking studies have also provided useful information for protection and management of tiger preserves in many other areas.

Pugmarks

Not all tiger research is as successful as the type carried out in Chitwan. One of the most important ongoing research projects, which is done on one level or another everywhere tigers are found, is census-taking, or getting an accurate population count. There has been a great deal of controversy surrounding the most commonly used method of counting tigers: tracking of pugmarks.

Each pugmark, or footprint, is unique to the individual tiger who created it, much like a human's fingerprints. In India these marks are used for the national tiger census, taken every five years. It is a massive undertaking. Ten thousand forest staff and up to one hundred thousand trained volunteers scour the jungle for pugmarks. They make plaster casts of the clearest ones, noting exact place and time of discovery. All the records are checked for duplicates and sent off to the Project Tiger headquarters for analysis. Indian trackers claim that they can determine many things from an individual pugmark: sex, weight, approximate age, when the tiger passed by, and sometimes even the exact identity of a particular tiger, based on individual peculiarities. All the sketched and plaster-cast pugmarks are recorded and categorized. For years now, this has been the preferred method of census-taking for most nations where the tiger is found.

Not everyone agrees, however, on the validity of these methods. Ullas Karanth, a wildlife biologist, says that even some of the more experienced of the ten thousand research employees are unable to correctly identify pugmarks. He bases this claim on the poor results of tests administered to

The pads of this young tiger's feet leave distinct impressions, or pugmarks, on the ground. India's Project Tiger keeps records of tiger pugmarks to track the movements of these animals and to take census counts.

a number of rangers requiring them to categorize known or previously identified pugmarks. It has also been suggested that the census results have even been falsified and inflated by park rangers and administrators in an effort to make themselves look better. Valmik Thapar, of the IUCN's Cat Specialist Group, states that his analysis of India's 1993 census indicates that the results could be off by as many as one thousand tigers. This notion is supported by studies of prey throughout India that indicate that there are not enough prey to support the number of reported tigers.

Hornocker project

Another well-known and somewhat controversial research project is carried out farther north on the Amur tiger. The Hornocker Wildlife Institute was founded by Maurice

Hornocker in 1992 at the Sikhote-Alin Biosphere Reserve in eastern Russia. The Hornocker project intends to study the range and habitat of the Amur tiger to come up with accurate population counts and recommendations for the future establishment and operations of viable Russian tiger preserves. When the project began, things looked grim for the northernmost tiger. Hard winters in the 1980s, combined with the dissolution of the Soviet Union and Russia's subsequent inability to cope with enforcing regulations, led to many cold and hungry local people hunting nearly all the deer and wild game in the preserve. This severely depleted the tiger's prey. At the same time, mining and logging threatened to destroy the tiger's home. From 1992 to 1994, between forty and sixty tigers were shot and sent to China each year, presumably to support the bone trade. In 1995, due in part to the findings of the Hornocker Institute, the

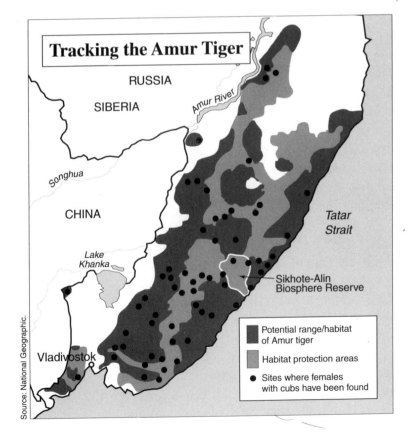

Tracking the Amur Tiger

RUSSIA

SIBERIA

Amur River

Songhua

CHINA

Tatar Strait

Lake Khanka

Sikhote-Alin Biosphere Reserve

Vladivostok

Potential range/habitat of Amur tiger

Habitat protection areas

● Sites where females with cubs have been found

Source: National Geographic.

Russian prime minister called for increased protection of the area and helped to better seal the Chinese borders.

Poaching began to drop significantly, and by 1996 Hornocker had completed the most extensive census survey ever conducted in the area. It came up with a grand total of 430 to 470 tigers throughout the Russian range. This turned out to be almost twice the previous estimate. The institute is now doing its best to keep these numbers up. A report it recently released points to the key factors in the survival of the Amur tiger: establishment of protected core breeding areas, buffer zones, biological corridors, and the regulation of logging and mining. There are groups, though, that feel the Hornocker project is a waste of resources and even unnecessarily invasive to the local tigers. Hornocker spends most of its resources on research, and these groups believe that the time and money would be better spent on rangers and equipment to protect the habitat now. They also feel the work should be discontinued because of the "uncomfortable" trap and release techniques employed. Similar to those at Chitwan, the cats are sedated and examined, but released in perfect health. It is a difficult and volatile issue. The Amur tiger still faces the immediate threat of poaching and habitat loss. Without the money to protect the tigers from these problems right now, they may be gone in a few years. However, if detailed studies of their needs are not conducted and acted upon over the next few years, they may never survive in the long run.

Zoos and breeding

Disagreement abounds over keeping tigers in captivity. Animal rights activists strongly believe that zoos and other facilities have no business keeping tigers at all. Many of these organizations, such as People for the Ethical Treatment of Animals (PETA), argue that tigers, as well as all other animals, belong only in the wild, and zoos should release their charges back into their natural habitat. This is not a realistic possibility, as the adult cats in zoos were never taught the survival skills they would need to exist in the wild. Some researchers also feel that zoos are wasting much-needed funds on captive breeding when, in their opinion, it is doing nothing to preserve the tigers in the wild. These arguments are countered by other groups and researchers who feel that having tigers in captivity is an absolutely vital part of any conservation effort. The primary reasons for keeping endangered animals in captivity are to provide a stable and healthy breeding environment and help educate the general public about the conservation issues facing these animals in the wild.

While the pristine jungles of Asia would undoubtedly make a better home for any tiger, the simple fact remains that these areas no longer exist on a large enough scale to support a viable and self-sustaining population of tigers. In a controlled environment, such as a zoo, the tigers are free

A zookeeper plays with two female tigers. Some experts believe keeping tigers in zoos ensures a healthy breeding population while allowing the public to learn more about the animal's endangerment.

from the pressures that plague their wild cousins. They receive all the food, protection from the elements, and veterinary care they would need to remain healthy and reproduce. Captive breeding of tigers has been very successful over the years. In fact, they breed so easily in captivity that many zoo tigers are kept on birth control to prevent surplus animals and inbreeding.

The Species Survival Plan (SSP) is a national program that controls and coordinates all tiger breeding in facilities accredited by the American Association of Zoos and Aquariums. Each subspecies has a designated "studbook" keeper who is in charge of making sure that all these zoos are maintaining safe and genetically diverse breeding practices. In this way, even if the wild tiger populations disappear completely, a large, stable, and viable population of tigers will still exist in captivity. The long-term plans of the SSP allow for continued captive breeding up to one hundred years from now, when a suitable and stable habitat will hopefully exist in the wild for these cats to return to.

Education

The second front on which zoos can help tigers is by raising the public awareness about their situation. The World Zoo Conservation Strategy (WZCS) estimates that 600 million people visit zoos annually. Most zoo-goers are casual visitors who gain the opportunity to learn about tigers—their natural history, conservation status, and ecological importance. Perhaps most important, according to the WZCS, the zoos permit people to have a personal encounter with these magnificent predators. Many conservation education specialists believe that this personal live connection can give people a newfound respect for and appreciation of the animal that is unavailable through any other medium. Theoretically, this experience would serve to inspire people to do their part to help save the tiger.

Zoos keep track of and utilize research conducted on wild populations to design more naturalistic and healthier exhibits for the tigers, as well as for other animals. Unfortunately, as with anything else in the world, money be-

A zoo visitor looks into the enclosure of a rare white tiger. Though captive tigers often have elaborate living quarters, some animal activists feel that it is cruel to limit the tiger's range.

comes the limiting factor. Zoos with wealthy benefactors can afford to build luxuriant miniature ecosystems for their cats, while many smaller, poorly funded zoos are forced to do the best with what they have. Fortunately, tigers are one of the more popular animals in zoos today and so are typically near the top of most zoos' lists for renovations and improvements.

In addition to the benefit for the casual zoo-goer, many facilities also have formalized education programs for school groups ranging from grade school to college. These programs are designed to heighten people's awareness of wildlife and the role humans must play in its survival. Whether all these programs and experiences inspire people to further educate themselves, donate money, volunteer for local conservation groups, or even become field researchers, they can be invaluable tools in promoting the need for action. The tiger's future may depend on it.

5

The Future

WILL THE TIGER survive and flourish into the next century? This is a question that occupies the minds of an ever-increasing group of researchers and conservationists who have dedicated their lives to the tiger's future. The answer still hangs in the balance. Perhaps the first question that needs to be asked is, Should we save the tiger?

There are people who feel the processes of survival of the fittest and extinction are natural phenomena. They argue that tampering with this is an unnecessary waste of resources. An enormous amount of time and money is dedicated to preserving the tiger and its habitat. Should so much energy be diverted away from humans in need to protect a species on its way out due to simple natural selection?

One factor to consider is that the tiger's decline is seen by most biologists as anything but natural. Countless species have come and gone throughout the earth's history, but the rate of extinction has increased a thousand-fold since humankind arrived on the scene. The human species is more adaptable than any that has come before it. As a result, it has flourished and moved into every habitat in the world, displacing all the creatures that had formerly occupied a diverse and interconnected variety of ecological niches. While this can be seen as the very successful progress of a species' development, it can also be viewed as a species growing unchecked, beyond the earth's capacity to support it. As humans burn out the earth's resources, including decimating animal species that form vital links in the food chain and energy web, they undermine the foundation of the very world in which they live.

Biologists realize the importance of preserving *complete* ecosystems. Every plant, animal, insect, and fungus serves an incalculable role in maintaining the delicate structure of the entire web of life. The average person does not know or care about the importance of the more "trivial" species. This is where the tiger can play a major role in conservation. People love tigers, and many are willing to donate their money to saving them. The tiger acts as a keystone

Because tigers are majestic beasts, environmentalists are hopeful that their beauty will inspire people to learn more about preservation of the earth's species and habitats.

species for its habitat. In other words, tigers are the main attraction of conservation efforts that result in the preservation of entire Asian regions. All the smaller and less "lovable" creatures of these areas benefit from the habitat protection aimed at the tiger, leading to the protection and stabilization of entire biospheres, or natural ecosystems. So, in effect, by saving the tiger, humans are saving entire ecological systems, and consequently the health of their world.

Problems at Ranthambhore

As far as public opinion is concerned, the world does seem to have given the go-ahead to save the tiger. The question then becomes, How? Over the last twenty-five years, there have been a number of initiatives to save the tiger. Some have been more successful than others, but all have their problems.

India's Ranthambhore National Park, in the desert state of Rajasthan, has for many years been one of the crowning achievements of Project Tiger. Today, it is one of the world's leading destinations for ecotourists wishing to glimpse a wild tiger.

In 1984, however, a devastating monsoon swept through the area, destroying trees and massive amounts of vegetation. The local people who depend almost exclusively on their cattle for survival were forced to swarm over the protected park property to graze their cattle and collect grasses. The result was a small war between the park's wardens and the local people. The local villagers set up blockades to keep the guards from coming upon their illegal grazing activities. When the two groups came into contact, there was often violence.

In one instance, locals rose up against the guards, attacking with stones and sheer numbers. The attack left one forester dead and several others seriously injured. On another occasion Fateh Singh Rathore, former director of Ranthambhore, was beaten almost to death by disgruntled villagers while he tried to stop them from grazing their cattle within the park's boundaries. These people who were

losing their livelihood and facing the very real threat of their own extinction saw the government's efforts to protect the tiger and its habitat as a slap in the face. They were fighting for their lives, and the government seemed more concerned with the tiger than their needs.

These regular skirmishes made effective control of the four-hundred-square-kilometer preserve a near impossibility. The end result of these conflicts was a severe upset in the balance of that ecosystem. The wild deer and antelope had almost nothing left to feed on after the villagers swept through. Many of them died, so the tigers were suddenly faced with much fewer prey. This handicap to the tiger's survival came right before the sudden poaching surge of the late 1980s. Weakened by a degraded habitat, the population took a nosedive when the demand for Oriental tiger remedies reached India. Similar problems with poaching and, more importantly, increased clashes between local villagers and the forestry staff were occurring all throughout Asia.

A running tiger splashes through Ranthambhore National Park. Despite the preserve's success, clashes with neighboring villagers over grazing rights and poaching incidents have taxed the strength and effectiveness of the game wardens.

Solutions at Ranthambhore

Rather than concede to the increasing swell of humans and cattle that teemed at its borders or continue to fight an uphill battle, the administration of Ranthambhore decided to attempt addressing the root of the problem. In 1988 the Ranthambhore Foundation was established (now affiliated with the Global Tiger Patrol) with the intention of setting up a program of sustainable development for the locals around the preserve to help them improve their livelihood on their own land.

Seven villages initially took part in the program. It was a massive undertaking focused on many different areas: growing trees for firewood, timber, and fodder for livestock; rehabilitating decimated grazing lands; providing new high-yielding cattle breeds adapted to stall feeding rather than grazing; marketing of milk; providing medical and family planning facilities as well as health education; organizing income; producing activities for women such as production and sale of native crafts; and providing environmental education for all, but most importantly for the children. So far, the program has been well received and very successful. The local people now take pride in their tigers and their ability to prosper along with them. The Global Tiger Patrol is now attempting to incorporate these successes into other areas throughout India.

The Amur tiger

The Siberian, or Amur, tiger has also met with some significant challenges in the last several years. Dale Miquelle of the Hornocker Institute reports that there are currently 450 tigers left in eastern Russia. They still have a very large range, although Amur tigers need larger individual territories because of low prey density. However, the biggest problem right now is hunting.

The old authoritarian regime that had ruled Russia for so many years may have been repressive to humans but it was very good at enforcing strict laws with severe penalties for tiger and habitat protection. With the collapse of communism and the changing leadership in Russia came terrible instability. The result is far more accessibility to tiger habitat for hunters. Virtually all adult males in eastern Russia are hunters, and now with the availability of firearms and the lack of permit enforcement, the tiger's prey base is being destroyed.

The breakdown of authority has also relaxed the monitoring of the Chinese borders, allowing the illegal trade of tigers to run unchecked. There is not much ecotourism in eastern Russia, so using that as leverage and financial incentive, as in Ranthambhore, carries little weight with the locals. In fact, officials have even discussed making the Amur available for limited high-priced sport hunting. The Amur's only salvation may come when the Russian government stabilizes itself and can afford to return some of its attention to saving its tigers.

Symposiums

The positive side of all the recent setbacks has been a reawakening of both professional and public interest in tiger conservation. It has been the catalyst for a maturing of conservation efforts worldwide, moving from a reactive approach to a preventive one.

Strict laws under Russia's Communist government once protected the Siberian tiger; however, as the nation's authority undergoes change, the tiger is once again being hunted.

In 1986, for example, at the Symposium on World Conservation in Minnesota, a Global Tiger Conservation Plan was established. This plan outlined several important areas of tiger conservation. Maintaining genetic diversity across all subspecies in both the wild and captivity was regarded as extremely important. This would allow the species to continue to grow in a natural manner. Linking of in situ (wild) and ex situ (captive) research programs, such as developing and implementing necessary biotechnology geared toward better management of agriculture and wild lands, was another point of focus. Because of the current disagreement about the exact number of tigers living in certain regions, the importance of accurate regional tiger population counts was highlighted. The final point urged the need to set specific criteria for when wild tiger populations should be moved into zoos.

A relaxing tiger stretches its tongue while yawning. The fate of these proud predators is now subject only to vigilant global conservation efforts.

This plan was innovative and sparked much-needed research and action. However, it failed to take into account several key factors, including the local human element, funding, and determining what exactly constitutes adequate tiger habitat.

In 1993 two more large symposiums were held: the International Symposium on the Tiger in New Delhi and the Amur Tiger: Problems Concerning Preservation of Its Population in Khabarovsk, Russia.

The tiger was a great focus for conservation in 1994. India initiated the Global Tiger Forum, attempting to involve the international community in its efforts by sharing its knowledge and progress. The United States passed the Rhino and Tiger Conservation Act, which attempts to provide financial assistance to conservation programs in areas where rhino and tiger populations are adversely affected. During the same year, Exxon and the National Fish and Wildlife Foundation joined together to begin the Save the Tiger Fund.

They promised $1 million a year for five years to education and research efforts focused on the tiger. Their website at www.5tigers.org is one of the best educational sites to explore information about the current status of the tiger.

Enlisting public support

Even the cover of the March 1994 issue of *Time* magazine had a huge portrait of a majestic tiger with the word "DOOMED" emblazoned across it. An enormous siege of articles in both wildlife and mainstream periodicals, as well as television shows, hotlines, websites, and classroom programs, flooded through the public consciousness that year and recruited a larger number of supporters for the cause than ever before. Enlisting public support is of crucial importance. According to John Seidensticker, "Ongoing information and education programs [are] a high priority. The public must be a partner in supporting the legal framework that protects the tiger, and footing much of the bill." Many zoos today are taking on that challenge by developing newer and more "marketable," or fun and exciting, education programs. The Bronx Zoo in New York cosponsors the Wildlife Conservation Society, which through donations raised by the zoo is able to conduct some of the world's leading conservation research in every corner of the world.

In addition, Tiger Global Animal Survival Plan recommends that zoos cooperate to provide $925,000 a year for ten years to in situ conservation efforts. The primary vehicle for this would be guest donations to adopt-a-park programs being made available at the zoos. It has suggested that the donations be divided up proportionally on a per-cat basis, so smaller zoos would not be overburdened with raising funds beyond their means. Regular progress reports would provide zoos with material for displays and marketing opportunities to gain new visitors and benefactors.

The work in education is far from complete. While planning a new tiger exhibit at the Smithsonian Institute's National Museum of Natural History, surveyors discovered that the general public is still grossly uninformed about the tiger.

The most recent large-scale forum occurred in February 1997. Named "Tigers: 2000," it was a symposium of many of the world's top tiger conservationists. The basic idea of the meeting was to have opposing factions of tiger conservation sit down and come to an agreement about the exact nature of the problem. Attempts to find a solution cannot begin until the problem itself has been accurately defined. By pooling all the efforts of captive breeders and researchers, in situ foresters and researchers, education specialists and political activists, a truly effective plan can be created and put into action. At the same time these larger groups will have more of an impact on convincing governments to cooperate and contribute funds. Disagreement and fragmentation between various groups all working to save the tiger can be counterproductive. Many groups still disagree about the best solutions to the problem of tiger preservation, but Tigers: 2000 took the first step by opening the door for an exchange of ideas and opinions.

New initiatives

There are currently a large number of new tiger conservation initiatives springing up all over the world. The World Wildlife Fund (WWF) and Wildlife Conservation Society have begun a project using satellite imagery to plot suitable tiger habitats in India, Indochina, and Indonesia. These scans will show the location of dense forested areas, but, unfortunately, they reveal nothing about what lives in them. Each individual area will have to be investigated to determine if there is enough prey to support a translocated tiger population. One British researcher wanted to take this a step further by tranquilizing and tagging every tiger in India with special equipment so they could all be tracked by satellite. This project, while bold, is extremely expensive and may never come to fruition.

Indian initiatives

A large part of the battle to save tigers revolves around money and political authority. Without these things all the good intentions in the world won't help a single tiger. New

Various organizations in India are trying to save the nation's tigers by strengthening protective measures and inducing sections of the public to give up their land-hungry agricultural livelihoods.

groups are coming together every day to raise funds and petition local governments. India is once again at the forefront of these initiatives. Tiger Link, a new Indian organization, recently managed to convince a large percentage of its nation's parliament to sign an appeal to the prime minister to strengthen the central government's tiger protection, much as it was in the days when Indira Gandhi was alive.

One of the largest programs to date involves the cooperation of the Global Environment Facility and the World Bank. They have joined together in a $67 million ecodevelopment program designed to reduce human pressure on five specific tiger preserves in India. The program intends to extend credit to local people to start up new nonagricultural livelihoods, as well as provide conservation agreements, specific programs for joint forest management, education, and conservation awareness. All these goals are aimed at promoting better living conditions for local people, so they will have less of a reason to impact the tiger and its habitat.

Chitwan profit sharing

A similar, smaller-scale project is being conducted by the WWF in Nepal's Chitwan National Park. The villagers around this park recently assisted in replanting and redeveloping several square miles of degraded forest. In exchange they were allowed to share in the income brought in by tourists in search of tigers. In one year, the local people earned $308,000. Just as important, several new tigers have moved into the area. This marks a true successful blending of expanding habitat and working with the local human population rather than against them.

Future areas

Overall, the world's tiger population has risen slightly in the last twenty years. However, it is easy to be lulled into a false sense of security. Current estimates put the global tiger population at somewhere between five thousand and seven thousand individuals. If all these animals lived in one connected habitat, they would be on their way to once again becoming a viable population. Unfortunately, most of these tigers live in approximately 160 individual and completely isolated areas spread across Asia. According to conservationist and researcher Eric Wikramanayake, each of these areas is home to an average of about thirty cats.

Wikramanayake's research has categorized all 160 areas into groups, based on their long-term viability as suitable tiger habitats. The twenty-five most promising areas were labeled level I tiger conservation units (TCUs). Twenty-one others were labeled level II, and sixteen were classified as level III. The rest were deemed unfit for TCU status, as they are considered to have very little chance of supporting tigers into the future. In theory, the higher the level assigned a particular area, the more resources will be devoted to protecting it and helping its resident tigers to survive. The report emphasized that strictly protected national parks and preserves make up only a small fraction of the designated TCUs, and efforts should be made to wisely manage all the areas, not just the ones in the public eye.

The future of the tiger is uncertain. Countless groups are working very hard to protect it, but there are just as many groups whose interests conflict with that of the tiger or its habitat. One could say that a war is being waged in the jungles of Asia. However, to date, the majority of the casualties have been its most unwitting participants: the tigers. Right now the tiger stands at the brink of extinction. Over the next twenty years, the actions of the world's 5 to 6 billion people will decide once and for all whether the tiger will continue to survive or pass from the earth forever.

Glossary

biosphere: Any region of earth that is occupied by living matter.

carnivore: A member of the order Carnivora, characterized by the possession of carnassial teeth designed like scissors to shear meat.

census: A count or tally of a specific population.

chuff: An auditory greeting used by tigers to communicate and convey recognition.

CITES: Convention on International Trade in Endangered Species. A regulatory group that decides, through the mutual agreement of its members, on international policies concerning trade in endangered species.

clear-cutting: Practice of felling all the trees in a section of forest at the same time.

ecosystem: A biologically balanced environment formed by the interaction of plants and animals.

ecotourism: The booming industry that provides nature-oriented vacations in national parks and reserves.

endangered species: A plant or animal species that is nearing extinction.

estrus: Hormonal breeding cycle that female tigers go through when they are ready to reproduce.

ex situ: Literally "out of its original place." Used to specify actions or research that takes place in captivity.

extinction: The complete and permanent elimination of a plant or animal species.

flehmen: The act of wrinkling the nose and opening the mouth to better take in and identify a scent mark left behind by another tiger.

genetic diversity: A healthy recombination of DNA, which allows a species to thrive and develop throughout time.

habitat: The locality or living place of a plant or animal.

in situ: Literally "in its original place." Used to specify actions or research that takes place in the wild.

IUCN: International Union for the Conservation of Nature. Organization that conducts research and makes recommendations on conservation issues.

keystone species: An animal that has the ability to shape or modify its habitat.

moratorium: A temporary ban or suspension of an activity such as hunting or trading.

national park: An area of wild habitat protected from development by a nation's government.

Panthera tigris: Scientific name for the tiger.

poaching: Illegal hunting or removal from private or protected lands.

prey base: The supply of suitable food items for the tiger in a given habitat.

pugmark: Term for tiger paw prints used to identify and tally tiger populations.

shikari: A Nepalese term for hunter.

SSP: Species Survival Plan. A plan drawn up by the American Association of Zoos and Aquariums to help ensure the future of selected species through tightly controlled captive breeding practices.

sustainable development: Utilizing an area's resources without destroying them.

Organizations
to Contact

Hornocker Wildlife Institute
University of Idaho
PO Box 3246
Moscow, ID 83845
(208) 885-6871
e-mail: hwi@uidaho.edu

The institute conducts long-term research on a number of threatened species and sensitive ecological systems, focusing on scholarly, creative efforts designed to make lasting contributions to our knowledge of the natural world.

IUCN/SSC Cat Specialist Group
Attn: Peter Jackson, Chairman
1172 Bougy
Switzerland
+41-21-808-6012

The Cat Specialist Group is an international panel of over 170 scientists, wildlife managers, and other specialists from 40 countries who have volunteered their expertise to the Species Survival Commission of IUCN. Its function is to provide IUCN, CITES, and governmental and nongovernmental organizations with advice on all matters concerning wild cats, including their status in nature, the threats they face, conservation requirements, and biology and natural history. The group also publishes a very informative newsletter to its members.

National Wildlife Federation (NWF)
1412 16th St. NW
Washington, DC 20036
(202) 797-6800
website: www.nwf.org

The NWF attempts to advance commonsense conservation policies through advocacy, education, and litigation in concert with affiliate groups across the country and throughout the world. It also publishes several informative, award-winning magazines, such as *International Wildlife*.

Ranthambhore Foundation
19 Kautilya Mark
Chanakyapuri
New Delhi 11021, India
+91-11-301-6261
e-mail: Tiger.linking@axcess.net.in

The long-term objectives of the foundation are to maintain the essential ecological balance necessary for humans to live in harmony with nature in the vicinity of Ranthambhore National Park and to undertake every possible measure necessary to ensure wildlife and forest conservation, especially for the tiger and its habitats. Recently, this group has also established Tiger Link, which seeks to incorporate its successes in all other parts of India.

Save the Tiger Fund
c/o National Fish and Wildlife Foundation
1120 Connecticut Ave. NW, Suite 900
Washington, DC 20036
(800) 5TIGERS
website: www.5tigers.org

This fund was established by the joint efforts of the Exxon corporation and the NFWF. Its goal is to save the tiger from extinction in the wild through the generous funding of a diverse and effective group of conservation projects. The fund has supported Ron Tilson's research in the rain forests of

Sumatra, the Hornocker Wildlife Institute, two antipoaching projects in India and one in Russia, as well as smaller-scale projects in Thailand and Cambodia. It also supports a number of education and captive breeding projects here in the United States. Its website provides access to one of the most comprehensive tiger information sites on the Internet.

United Nations Environment Programme (UNEP)
DC2-0803
United Nations
New York, NY 10017
(212) 963-8093
website: www.unep.org

UNEP's mandate is to provide leadership and encourage partnership in caring for the environment by inspiring, informing, and enabling nations and peoples to improve their quality of life without compromising that of future generations. It is a very active participant in a wide variety of international research and action plans.

Wildlife Conservation Society (WCS)
Attn: Tiger Campaign
185th St. & Southern Blvd.
Bronx, NY 10460
(718) 220-6891

Dedicated to preserving the earth's wildlife and ecosystems, the WCS combines scientifically based conservation efforts in the field with captive propagation of endangered species, and provides environmental education for local, national, and international audiences. Its Tiger Campaign, launched in 1993, attempts to focus a large amount of attention on issues surrounding the tiger and its preservation.

World Wildlife Fund (WWF)
1250 24th St. NW
Washington, DC 20037
(202) 293-4800
website: www.wwf.org

Established in 1961, the WWF is one of the most well-known conservation groups in the world. It helps to create and protect wildlife reserves throughout the world, and develops public education programs, investigates poaching and smuggling, and attempts to reconcile human needs with conservation through research and active programs.

Suggestions for Further Reading

Tom Brakefield, *Kingdom of Might: The World's Big Cats*. Stillwater, MN: Voyager Press, 1993.

Philip Gourevitch, "No More Tigers," *Outside*, February 1995.

Peter Jackson, *Endangered Species: Tigers*. Secaucus, NJ: Chartwell Books, 1991.

Eugene Linden, "Tigers on the Brink," *Time*, March 28, 1994.

Mel Sunquist, "What I've Learned About Tigers," *International Wildlife*, November/December 1997.

Valmik Thapar, *The Tiger's Destiny*. New York: Eddison/Sadd Editions, 1994.

Geoffrey C. Ward, "Tigers in Trouble," *National Geographic*, December 1997.

Works Consulted

"Action Plan to Save the Siberian Tiger," *Cat News—IUCN Cat Specialist Group*, Autumn 1994.

"A Bomb Explodes in the Battle Against Tiger Poachers," *Cat News—IUCN Cat Specialist Group*, Autumn 1994.

Stanley Breeden, "In the Spell of the Tiger," *International Wildlife*, September/October 1992.

Peter Jackson, "Man-Eaters!" *International Wildlife*, November/December 1985.

"Killed for a Cure: The Tiger Bone Trade," *Cat News— IUCN Cat Specialist Group*, Autumn 1994.

Linda Litchfield, "Save the Tiger," *Zoolife*, Summer 1991.

Rupert Matthews, *How They Live: Tigers*. Bdd Promotional Book Co., 1990.

Peter Matthiessen, "Tiger in the Snow," *New Yorker*, January 6, 1997.

"Modeling the Effects of Tiger Poaching," *Science News*, December 16, 1995.

Kristin Nowell and Peter Jackson, eds., *Status Survey and Conservation Action Plan: Wild Cats*. Gland, Switzerland: IUCN, 1996.

Kevin Schafer and Martha Hill, "The Logger and the Tiger," *Wildlife Conservation*, May/June 1993.

John Seidensticker, "Saving the Tiger," *Wildlife Society Bulletin*, Spring 1997.

Lee Server, *Tigers: A Look into the Glittering Eye*. Stanford, CT: Longmeadow Press, 1993.

"Siberia Undercover," *Time*, September 4, 1995.

Billy Arjan Singh, "Save the Tiger—the Last Ditch," *Tiger Information Center Website*, January 10, 1996.

"A Stick to Save Tigers," *Time*, April 18, 1994.

Valmik Thapar, *Tiger: Portrait of a Predator*. New York: Eddison/Sadd Editions, 1989.

Geoffrey C. Ward, "India's Intensifying Dilemma: Can Tigers and People Coexist?" *Smithsonian*, November 1987.

Daniel Zatz, "Last Favor for a Missing Tiger," *International Wildlife*, July/August 1993.

Index

Picture Credits

About the Author

Stuart P. Levine received his bachelor's degree in behavioral psychology at the State University of New York at Binghamton, and his associate's degree in wildlife education/animal management at Moorpark College in southern California.

He spent several years working with a variety of animals, from tigers to fruit bats, at a park in northern California. While there, he served as a wildlife educator, presenting programs to grammar and middle schools geared toward heightening young people's awareness of wildlife and wild habitats.

Though a native New Yorker and a Californian at heart, Levine currently resides in Orlando, Florida, where he continues to work at spreading environmental awareness at Disney's Animal Kingdom.